PASSIVITY

For the Thousands

PASSIVITY

Between Indifference and Pacifism

Alexandra Tryanova & Pascal Gielen
visuals: Polina Frank

valiz

Do we do this in the name of peace? In contrast to violence, writing is perhaps one of the most pacifist acts. After all, anyone who can express something with words does not have to use violence to enforce their view. Arguments can transform brute force into authority. But using words rather than deeds—does that not also testify to passivity and resignation? The symbolic inversion of true violence? Writing as passive aggression. Is pacifism complicit in war? Is there blood on our hands? We have wrestled with it constantly. When does our own pacifism become resignation, or even cowardice? We have written about it and in it—wavering between pacifism and indifference. What is going on in Europe? What is going on with Europe? What is going on in ourselves?

Alexandra Tryanova & Pascal Gielen
Antwerp, March 2023

CONTENTS

MY COUNTRY

PASCAL: You immediately feel at home in some countries. Ukraine is one of those countries for me. Of course, this is a completely imaginary and subjective, even visceral feeling. After all, I don't know the language, culture or history of the country. So is it because of the people you meet there? The warmth, the fun, the mutual interest, the exchanged glances? Possibly. But I also worked in the Netherlands for ten years, with exceptionally nice colleagues, and I have kept several friendships from that time. Yet, even though they speak the same language as me, I never felt at home there. The culture there seems fundamentally different from that of my home country, Belgium. In any case, it made me realise that feeling at home in a country depends on more than just the people you meet there. Culture is much harder to grasp and is much more than the sum of a few relationships with individuals.

You came to live in Belgium shortly before the war. May I ask how you feel here? Is there a difference in how people here treated you before the war and now? And is there a difference in how you saw your own country of Ukraine before the war and now?

ALEXANDRA: Firstly, I agree that feeling at home somewhere else largely depends on your personal emotional experience and the people you meet. When you get that entirely subjective and emotional 'click' of recognition, you experience a place as home. But are we talking about a place or a country? I was recently wondering what my special relationship is with Istanbul, a city where I've spent a lot of time and where I feel at home. But can I transfer this feeling to the whole of Turkey, which I know less about? I'm not so sure, because my feeling is also bound up with the city's many layers of history and its local aesthetics. I used to see this more through a Greek lens, as a particular attitude towards *polis* or province. Today my attitude has changed considerably. You can never understand what suffering is until your own homeland is bombed. And, on top of that, it is difficult when you are physically safe abroad, while your

loved ones and all the other innocent people are still in constant danger of death. At a time like that, you suddenly feel every square inch of your country as part of your own body.

When I left Ukraine in autumn 2021 to study in Belgium, I wanted to live a kind of nomadic life, to gather experiences and develop professionally on an international level. To be honest, I didn't feel very safe in my home country because of the Russian military manoeuvres on the Ukrainian border and the country's political situation. That also galvanised my thoughts about other possible paths. After all, the war had already been going on for six years when I came to Belgium. Anyway, after coming here, I mostly moved in the art-world circles. I was fascinated by the varied and dynamic scene here. Unfortunately, by December, this entertaining and inspiring image began to fade quickly, as all attention shifted to the news from Ukraine, where the smell of war was already strong. I remember how we awkwardly started using the word 'war' when I talked to my mother about our future, and that gave me a terrible feeling of helplessness.

Aside from all the comforts of Belgium, and its unique atmosphere, the people I've met here are the most important thing for me. So many thoughtful and empathetic people, amazingly talented and from so many different spheres and backgrounds. They surrounded me with so much care, as if we had known each other for centuries. Surprises come from all angles: there's always someone around who has a grandmother who's from my hometown of Odesa. Or you start collaborating with a group of local artists who don't look like activists at first. Only after several meetings do you find out that they helped send ambulances to Ukraine. Another time, you are amazed by a beautiful scene in the hammam when Moroccan women unexpectedly start singing in chorus. All that is Belgium for me now. I don't think I've had any unpleasant experiences here. At least not until recently, when I ran into two Russians at the swimming pool, comparing notes on how they had escaped mobilisation. Thinking that I couldn't understand them, they started discussing my appearance in a disgusting way. I hadn't heard such nonsense since I was in Riga last year, and this unpleasant experience somehow shook my sense of security here.

You ask if there is a difference in my attitude before the war and now. Definitely, yes, because I receive a lot of support and empathy. After everyone was initially shocked by the level of brutality, the people around me wanted to help and made a personal effort to do so. However, some were also afraid of how Ukrainians might behave, what their reactions and emotions might be. Fear is often caused by ignorance. Who are they? What country is it? How do you behave when someone standing here before you is completely absorbed in a war taking place two thousand kilometres away? What kind of help is needed? It took a while for everyone here to understand that we are not fleeing poverty but missiles. By now, probably everyone knows Ukraine a little better, and even something of its history. You can tell that most people today are more or less used to having Ukrainians here. But they also have difficulty understanding us as victims because it is unclear what trauma we've suffered. In any case, this is a rather questionable and limited approach, since it reduces us to victims. What I'm trying to say is that Ukrainians do not need sympathy, they need solidarity. Now, after a series of massive Russian attacks, the international community has dramatically increased military aid to Ukraine. I hope this calms the voices of the so-called pacifists who are pressing for arms supplies to be stopped.

I used to see national concepts as a retrogression, but that view has quickly washed away with the blood that is now flowing in my country. Today, I know that my country is the land where people sing together, sheltering in a metro station during the bombing. I don't know any other nation on the planet that would behave like that.

PASCAL: The distinction you make between sympathy and solidarity intrigues me. I sometimes get the impression that European politics and attitudes towards war are based on a combination of compassion, and strategic and economic considerations. Or rather that, because of economic considerations, the politics of solidarity gets no further than sympathy. Belgium's refusal to boycott the Russian diamond trade is a clear sign of this. That, combined with the screening of the television programme *Ukraine 12-12* by the leading Flemish media outlets, points to a curiously motivated pacifism. The TV show was a model of pathetic, dare I even say paternalistic, pity. It reminded me a bit of the way the Catholic Church acted towards poor believers for decades, or how it dealt with the colonies. Although the church gave aid to the poor and provided education to the indigenous populations, it usually refused to address the problem of structural poverty and the colonial exploitation policies. As a result, poverty and the prevailing power relations persisted. The church thus legitimised the colonial system.

Europe's policy of non-intervention is much like that old Christian attitude. Europe does show solidarity with Ukraine, but does it also dare use violence to break the existing geopolitical power relations between Russia and Ukraine once and for all? For now, I see no movement in that direction, which to me indicates a pacifism based on sympathy rather than solidarity. It also testifies to a kind of political resignation. As if nothing can be done about the existing geopolitical balance of power anyway, even with a powerful ally like the United States. But I'm not a specialist in international politics, so it's difficult for me to judge the specific situation. I can only look at it through a cultural lens. When I do so, what strikes me is the discourse about the war, which also expresses solidarity. I call it misplaced pacifism with a paternalistic flavour, whose implicit overtones are 'West is best' and 'Look at Russia now. We were right all along.' This attitude is deeply rooted in Western culture, and it has now had confirmation that it was absolutely right as far as the Russian aggressor was concerned.

This also brings me back to what you said about the role of culture. Culture has always played a role in nation state building and national politics. For example, in our book *The Art of Civil Action*, the Russian writer and curator Ilya Budraitskis argues that Russia's Ministry of Culture is part of the Ministry of Defence. Cultural manifestations can thus easily become part of nationalist politics and even of a well-conceived geopolitical strategy. But culture can also play a positive role. Singing together, as you say. It generates courage and a powerful sense of solidarity. But I wonder what trauma this war will leave in Ukrainian culture. And whether art can help process this trauma. How do you think culture can play a role in rebuilding Ukraine? When politicians talk about reconstruction, they usually talk about infrastructure and economy—seldom about culture. Whereas I think it is in culture that the wounds are deepest, and traumas are passed on down many generations. On top of that, economic and infrastructure problems can be solved much faster.

How do you see the role of artists in this? What role do they play in the war now, and what role could they play in rebuilding Ukraine?

ALEXANDRA: It's interesting that you mention the Christian attitude to war. Christianity puts mercy before justice. That explains, for instance, why Pope Francis often promotes ideas that are contrary to the needs and will of Ukrainians fighting a bloody aggressor. Pope Francis has made many unacceptable proposals such as taking the interests of the Russian Federation into account, because 'Putin may have been provoked'. He literally spoke of Russia's war with Ukraine as a typical bilateral conflict, not as Russian aggression. That is how a pro-Russian agenda spreads through the vast global Christian network.

But let's get back to art. I avoid generalisations when it comes to artists. Now, during the active phase of the war, with no end in sight yet, Ukrainian artists are playing many roles. They are serving in the army; rescuing people and animals from occupation; sorting through the rubble after shelling; fundraising; driving cars bought for the Ukrainian army across Europe directly to the front lines; buying grenades out of their artistic fees and writing their dearest wishes for the enemy on them. They are documenting war crimes; opening exhibitions; speaking in venues that were previously barely accessible to them and breaking through the wall of prejudice and excuses of the 'not everything is so clear cut' kind. Artists are explaining their country's history and demonstrating the colonial nature of the people of Ukraine's oppression; providing psychological support to war victims; and caring for people they know and people they don't. They are trying to be OK. They're going missing and dying, just like thousands of other Ukrainians. The current phase could perhaps be called a time of active care, where it is not so much a professional vocation that inspires people as a personal moral obligation. Some may be immersing themselves in their artistic practice and continuing to work and build a career. Others are finding it challenging to think about art right now. In general, constant stress significantly deadens the empathy for art. This became painfully evident among artists abroad after the outbreak of war. Their keen interest and enthusiasm changed overnight. They suddenly looked at the art world around them with complete detachment.

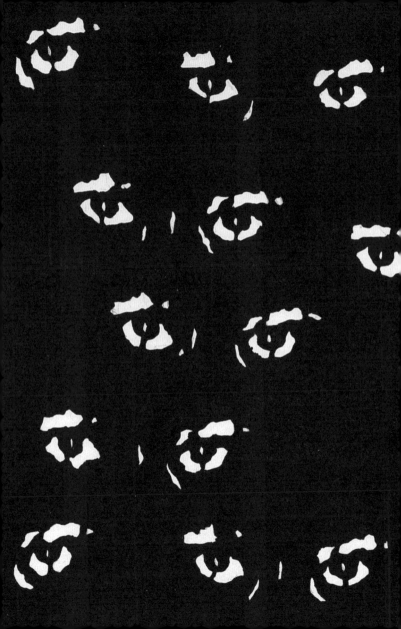

Clearly, in the post-war period, there is great potential for art to initiate systemic change. By that, I mean that the political imagination of artists has a chance to materialise in practice and lead to a breakthrough in the creation of equality, diversity, greater access to culture, critical thinking and the promotion of public discussion in general. The optimistic point of view is that art in Ukraine can reach a whole new level of interaction with its audience thanks to the shared experience and mutual recognition. But let's look at today's actual statistics. Part of the Ukrainian art community remains in Ukraine, while another part has moved to a safe place. This is giving rise to entirely different experiences, and in my view this difference can lead to strong contradictions in the future. When we talk about rebuilding culture after the war, we usually first rely on institutions that can offer relevant education and presentation opportunities. Today, however, the architecture of relations between political power and cultural institutions is far from balanced, and this may provoke additional misunderstanding. Furthermore, there are a large number of institutions that lack stability. Nevertheless, there are leaders in all cultural fields, and they will be the first to launch post-war education and culture programmes, supported by foreign partners or reparations. But what kind of experience will these institutions' programme makers have? Who will teach at the academies? What will be the balance between professors' and students' experiences? And how relevant will this dialogue be to the broader art discourse? This really worries me, because I imagine that, in the next thirty years, Ukrainian art will be mostly concerned with the war and war experiences, and I don't think that will be particularly conducive to fostering international dialogue. I'm scared that Ukrainian contemporary art will become isolated then.

Meanwhile, since the beginning of the war, a certain taboo has appeared in public debate in Ukrainian society against criticising the authorities so that general unity can be preserved with victory as the sole aim. This is more than understandable. But how long can this 'extension spring' hold? There is such a thing as metal fatigue. Unity and unanimity can simply snap and break at some point.

At the same time, the mechanisms of public administration and funding for culture and education—important starting points for identity building—require special attention. Funding for these sectors has now been reduced as far as possible, entirely predictably.

Yet even in 2021, before the war, there was a significant decline in subsidies. Even now, during the war, the demolition of one of the film industry's most important institutions is continuing. The Ukrainian State Film Agency plans to reorganise the Dovzhenko Centre, which means breaking up the National Film Archive. The Centre has been consistently engaged in the preservation, research and popularisation of Ukrainian cinema since 1994. It is Ukraine's largest and only internationally recognised film archive, and it holds more than 10,000 Ukrainian and foreign feature films, documentaries and animated films, more than 24,000 archival documents on the history of Ukrainian film and more than 400 museum pieces. Ukraine will lose its place in the International Federation of Film Archives if the institution is reorganised. FIAF has already reminded President Zelensky of the importance of preserving the collection and activities of the Dovzhenko Centre. Now the State Film Agency has appointed Julia Kazhdan as the centre's acting director-general, as a 'crisis manager'. Before landing this job, Julia moved in very different professional circles: she was the founder of a kennel club and a practising hypnotherapist. It is precisely such episodes that will obviously require the collective participation of cultural professionals since only they have an in-depth understanding of the context of the situation, expertise, and, hopefully, a knowledge of how to unite people in direct action.

PASCAL: Your story about the Dovzhenko Centre's film archive sounds cynical, even a little scary. It seems that what is presented as a joke in the Ukrainian satirical TV series *Servant of the People*— that is to say, incapable people being placed in important positions— is actually being carried out, only not as a joke any more. Ominously, fact and fiction are merging, just as in Jean Baudrillard's hyperreality. The replacement of experts by managers who can manage anything—be it universities, hospitals, kennels, nurseries or museums—is a trend that we in Western Europe also have to witness in sorrow. In the book *Institutional Attitudes*, we describe this trend metaphorically as 'the world becoming flat'. It means that a given institution can easily be compared quantitatively (participation figures, the number of hospital beds, student numbers, etc.) with an entirely different institution. I believe this development belongs to a 'de-democratisation movement' that ultimately supports only one ideology: neoliberalism.

Again, it is striking how this 'managerial realism' uses figures and above all budget deficits to silence any opposition and any substantive criticism. While, in the book *Institutional Attitudes*, intellectuals such as Chantal Mouffe still pinned their hopes on cultural institutions to counter this anti-democratic movement, I fear that the management virus has struck there too now. In the long run, this generates a resigned cynicism among staff and experts such as curators, artists, teachers and researchers. 'As long as we tick off the numbers and meet the targets and quotas, they'll leave us alone.' The result, in other words, is a general passivity, but one concealed behind a hyperactivity of accountability in audits, self-assessments and accreditations. It makes professionals too active to actually act. They increasingly occupy themselves with things they are not trained for and that they have no drive for. The result is massive burnout and loss of staff.

I can imagine that a war would silence criticism of such a regime just as well. But my experience of the Ukrainian cultural sector shows that there is still enough critical mass there to turn the tide, I hope. It may sound a bit inappropriate to say this, but I think a war can even wake people up and make them aware of what life is really all about. It is not bureaucratic accountability that energises us, that makes us create and enjoy life. It is love, solidarity and an obsessive dedication that motivates us and keeps us motivated. At least, I have the impression that art and politics, artists and activists are much more interlinked in the former Eastern European countries than in Western and certainly than in Northern Europe. For years here, under the guise of 'artistic autonomy', the arts sector has looked down its nose at anything that smelt of politics, activism and social engagement. In short, the cultural sector has hidden behind a veil of political indifference for years. Even though the tide is now turning, it may be too late for the 'former West'. How do you see things for Ukraine? Do you think artists will play an active role in rebuilding a democracy? When I was in Ukraine—and in Russia, for that matter—I got the feeling that the people there looked up enormously to Western Europe. But do you think they are also mindful of the 'de-democratisation spiral' the 'former West' finds itself in? To put it another way, could the first-mover disadvantage apply in

Ukraine? I mean, that artists and other cultural professionals in Ukraine learn from how things are going wrong in the rest of Europe (and the United States)?

ALEXANDRA: I completely understand your idea of the 'management virus' that subverts work processes for the sake of performance indicators, and of course I recognise how damaging this trend is. This certainly occurs in Ukraine too, but corruption is often the underlying reason there, so people try to cover up destructive reorganisations with statements about inefficiency. In the case of the Dovzhenko Centre, the reason for the attack on the institution is the desire of the authorities, represented by the ministry, to find another use for the building that houses the centre. A new residential complex is being built right next door, in fact, along with retail space and other accessories of the carnival of consumption. The authorities are driving a gulf between themselves and the cultural community with these despicable manoeuvres and undermining any hope for change. This will undoubtedly result in specialists no longer wanting to work in Ukraine. Despite the war, the cultural authorities continue to believe that they can develop their corrupt strategies even further, which makes me completely despair, personally. Because all you can hope for in the current situation is the strength of protest. But in a state of war, with the number of professionals who have moved abroad, this does not seem to work. On the other hand, if you compare the film industry to other cultural sectors, you can see that this community is perhaps the most professional, has extensive connections with colleagues abroad and knows how to handle a budget. So the response that has emerged in this area may set a good example for the protection of cultural heritage and their own rights for other cultural fields.

In my opinion, Ukrainian artists still idealise Western cultural systems a great deal. But of course there are still a few artists who continue to look critically at the way things work abroad. I'm thinking not only of the artists who identify with the leftist movement but also those who have a rare gift for independent thinking. Constructing a critical stance requires a lot of curiosity and personal experience, along with an understanding of history and foresight generally. To learn from something, you need to

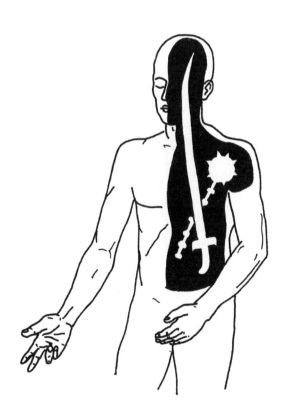

exchange experiences, and I think that, for the majority of Ukrainian artists, this is still more of an idea than a practical reality. Many 'Western' practices are adopted in Ukraine only as window dressing: their content is lost. Ukrainians have taken on the things that are obviously visible or tangible. That acts like a low-resolution copy. It is interesting to note that, in Ukrainian, and in Russian, a photocopy is called a 'xerocopy' because the first copiers were produced there by Xerox. The language picked up the company name rather than something describing the machine's actual function.

But what's good is that Ukrainians are not very prejudiced against activism and political participation compared to how you describe Western attitudes to it. Even more than that, a clear and active position seems to be an essential part of the artistic figure in Ukraine. The obscurantism that was possible before the war is no longer possible in this day and age. So I believe that art and cultural participation can certainly play a role in bringing change in Ukraine.

PASCAL: Let me end with a completely different question. From the start of the war, I have also been in contact with several colleagues and acquaintances in Russia. Although I must say that this 'open' contact has become increasingly difficult. Perhaps it has something to do with the cultural milieu I found myself in in Russia, but there, too, I noticed a lot of opposition to the war and to Putin himself— long before the war began, by the way. I can imagine that cultural relations between Ukraine and Russia have soured at the moment— that there are deep wounds in both countries' cultural sectors and in the relations between them. Do you see a role for artists and other cultural workers in getting these relations back on track after the war? More generally, do you think culture could play a role in rebuilding peaceful relations?

ALEXANDRA: It's a real challenge for me to accept the approach expressed in your question. The colleagues and acquaintances many of us have in Russia are small exceptions in the whole social sphere. There is just not enough energy in this group, it cannot be converted into real action. *C'est la vie.* And I would contend that 'soured' scarcely corresponds to the current reality. Cultural relations between Ukraine and Russia have simply stopped. But Russian gas still runs through Ukrainian pipes. I also think we should be very careful with the expression 'both countries'. Do we really need this construct? How did it come about and why do we use it? Still, despite all the obstacles, Russian artists have a whole set of tools for decolonisation work. And I will only welcome projects that have that commitment.

SOCIETAL FATIGUE

Perhaps one of a sociologist's greatest sins. In the past ten years, I have barely touched a newspaper. I do watch the TV news daily, but I remember almost nothing from it. This puts me at a considerable disadvantage. Don't ask me who won the Tour de France or the Queen Elisabeth Competition. Or the name of the Ukrainian foreign minister, or the trendiest Belgian chef. The new rector of the Free University of Brussels? I should know. I do know the old one, but then she often appeared on TV. I had to learn from my eldest son that I'm a hipster. I may not have a beard, but I do drink buckets of oat milk. Until a few months ago, I thought squash was the top indoor sport. But it turns out it's been padel for quite some time. There are all sorts of things that pass you by when you don't read any newspapers. You won't be surprised to learn that quizzes are not for me. I'm never going to win any game shows.

However, we do get a paper. My girlfriend reads it online every day and in print at the weekend. So I am regularly reprimanded with a smile. 'Really, Mr Sociologist ...' or, worse: 'Really, Mr Professor, how do you not know that ... how do you still not know that this person is ...?'

Not that the world doesn't interest me. Certainly, the newspaper makes me curious. When the print version is out on the kitchen table at the weekend, I do pluck up the courage to read a bit of it over her shoulder. But mostly I go out of my way to avoid it. So then I have to miss out on it all. That Ilja Leonard Pfeijffer is enjoying being at home for the first time in his life. That Serena Williams is a superstar who is bigger than her sport. It doesn't pass me by that the persistent heat is making farmers sweat. Or that the teacher shortage is acute. Because I see that on TV. Don't get me wrong. It's not the banality of the news that keeps me away from newspapers. Television wallows in much more triviality. Even the news on the public networks. I can handle non-news, personal anecdotes and frivolous trivia quite well. Otherwise, I would have left Facebook long ago. Although I'm feeling increasingly uncomfortable on there too.

No, it is not the superficiality or the banality. So where does this newspaper phobia come from? I know the symptoms well. Newspaper journalism succeeds in constantly badgering me. News reports just won't let me go. A television news story evidently flashes by too quickly to really grab me. A newspaper can do that. And, strangely enough, that gets on my nerves. As if my responsibilities are relentlessly being appealed to. My shortcomings are pointed out. I am reproached for my inactivity. I should have been here or there. I should have gone to that exhibition or that concert. Also, help! The world is on fire. Do something! Now! React! Roll your sleeves up! Right away! Protest! Write an opinion. At least sign that petition. Maybe I read a newspaper too much like a manifesto. A rousing pamphlet. Insurgent language. Perhaps even an order.

That must be it. The permanent call to action as a painful confrontation with my own passivity. Television lets me resign myself to this. The newspaper does not. Instead, it accuses me of non-action. Possibly even apathy. At the very least aloofness. Is that behind my internal conflict? A matter of conscience? The battle with my own desire to be left alone. My disagreeable wish to distance myself from the world? To escape from it. Am I perhaps suffering from a pathological form of social fatigue? A thorny question. Especially for a sociologist.

However, commitment is not entirely foreign to me. I also enjoy meeting 'my' community. But I prefer to do that in books. Eight hundred words on some issue badger me. Two hundred pages on the same issue bring me some peace. With the newspaper, and online, I skip like a stone across the water; with a book, I dive in deep. Yet I am not concerned with depth. What is important to me is temporality. It brings serenity. 'Lassitude'. A book forces you to take your time; a newspaper makes you spring hastily into action.

Now, whether newspaper or book, it mainly teaches me that language does something to me. Not so much the content as the mass. The materiality. The rhythm. Not only the spirit but also the corpus of language defines my mind. And my relationship to my surroundings. It is as if the rhythm of language makes me resonate with the world. Even if the content is the same, a newspaper conditions me differently from a book. It also literally puts me in a different condition. The two make me quiver and sometimes quake with the world in a completely different way.

I'm not too keen on stimulus-response theory. At least not when it comes to our social behavioural interactions. But newspapers and social media did make me understand Ivan Pavlov better. His push for a physiological social theory. What newspapers and social media taught me is that signs, words and images act on us like kinetics. Societies form complex conglomerations of reflexes. Language stimuli generate mental responses, and the nature of the stimuli moulds cultural automatisms. This cultural reflex theory becomes more convincing when we look at how language, including figurative language, shapes our society today. And I am not talking so much about the content of that language as about the way it is presented. The rhythm, timbre, variety and speed. Sign-stimuli, whether sounds, words or images. The flow of stimuli determines the rhythm of life and the social dynamics of a society. That certainly counts for our current attention regime. Like Pavlov's dogs, stimuli can make an entire society drool. Even what we focus on and how long we can hold that focus is partly shaped by the rhythm of the media. In other words, a society relies on culture, signs and language. To use Marxist jargon, like the relations of production, they determine the foundation of a society. The latter hastily browses through them nowadays. To the utter amazement of his communist comrades, Joseph Stalin defended this thesis as early as 1950 in *Pravda*. Language is no mere superstructural phenomenon. Stalin, of course, knew better than anyone else what a few words can do to a human life.

It appears that Vladimir Putin has understood that message only too well. If you mix Pavlov's insights with Stalin's, you immediately see where the 'free' West's weakness and blind spot lie. The exuberant West is trapped in a language, in newspapers and social media that constantly badger its people, politicians and businesses. A world that, along with Francis Fukuyama, arrogantly places itself at the end of history does not need a utopia. It no longer sees a distant future. That world only knows and recognises the short-term perspective. A society of that ilk knows how to make a profit now—financially or electorally. But it does not understand how to capitalise in say a hundred years from now. Within that limited time horizon, hysteria and panic rule. The political arsenal is reduced to mere tactical thinking. Like a reflex logic. Always reacting quickly. Action and reaction. A wrong decision is better than a slow decision:

that was the management advice of a former Google CEO.

Putin is in a different temporal logic. He took twenty-two years to prepare his stratagem. To take control of German gas together with some of his old Stasi friends. Thereby, in effect, partly controlling their consumer society. But Putin also knows only too well that he is risking his own life with that game. Only a strategist dares such a long-term policy, not a tactician. Putin is therefore not aiming for a good result in the upcoming election polls. His goal is a tomb next to Lenin's. In other words, he is betting on an afterlife. That is to say, a life in the history books. Books! Not newspapers, and even less social media.

Books. It always amazed me on tour in Russia and Ukraine how many books still have a public life there. You see them in the metro, and on trains and buses. Certainly, they have to compete with smartphones there, too. But books are still much more prevalent there than here. On the radio and television too. Journalists still refer to them. And I'm not talking about cookery books. You will even still hear an occasional quote from Marx on the prime time news there. As well as references to writers and poets. This is the book culture Putin grew up in. So I wouldn't be at all surprised if it defined his time horizon. The Western media say Putin's face radiates indifference. Like that of a psychopath. I find his icy gaze mostly conveys endless patience. Paradoxically, such a gaze discerns the impossibility of action in all our ego and hyperactivity. This is perhaps what a newspaper and especially social media culture can learn from a book culture. The lesson that the *former East* can spell out to the *former West*. We are too active to actually act. *Much ado about nothing*. Beneath all our hysteria lurks a real passivity. Hyperactive resignation. Manic societal fatigue.

NOT A HIPPY COMMUNE

A week after the Russian invasion, Ukrainian writer and photographer Yevgenia Belorusets wrote in her war diary: 'I keep getting emails and messages telling me to be a pacifist. Ukrainians have never provoked a war, never wanted or supported a war. The values of pacifism are among the most important values of my country. I grew up with a saying: "The most important thing is that there be no war".'[1] The harrowing experiences of those born before and during World War II are deeply embedded in my family history and in the culture of dealing with the past. In my experience, echoed by many Ukrainians, veterans rarely spoke about the war and avoided questions about it. Some of the decisive battles of that war took place on the territory of modern Ukraine, and civilian and army losses amounted to ten million. That is more than any Allied or Soviet country, including Russia.

During the violent missile attacks on Ukraine, Yevgenia, like many others, stayed in her home in Kyiv, risking her own life. Simultaneously, she had to fend off other attacks of an epistolary nature. Foreign colleagues urged her to remain a pacifist and lay down her arms. This is practically the same as inviting victims to cease any resistance and suffer their sad fate. Such people have barely developed any sensitivity to the powerful and righteous impulse of Ukrainians to protect themselves from deadly attacks. They are stubbornly guided by the principles of pacifism and anti-militarism. But pacifism is blind to tragedy. Its adherents are barely aware of their own privileges. A pacifist is a rare beast in a bomb shelter.

It seems to me that the current polemic around pacifism is a product of conceptual confusion. Pacifism itself is a great thing, but it does not presuppose mere passivity. Pacifism is not a response that avoids terrorism. Defending a commitment to peace sometimes requires resisting with force. Ritual sacrifices do not stop war, or attacks on a democracy. So we are seeing something else under the veneer of pacifism. It is concealing other values. In fact, so-called pacifist views often correspond perfectly to Russian propaganda narratives. And they are seasoned with ignorance of the region's history and geography.

It is no challenge at all to uphold your principles and beliefs when you are a great way off from the war zone and comfortably ignorant of the crimes of Russian imperialism. In the past thirty years alone, Russia has occupied Moldova, launched or supported wars in Georgia, Chechnya, Syria, Libya and Ukraine, and effectively supported the dictatorial regime in Belarus.

Let me remind you, for instance, of the shocking open letter in May 2022 from German intellectuals to Chancellor Olaf Scholz asking him not to deliver heavy weapons to Ukraine. Surprisingly enough, there were no experts on Eastern Europe among the signatories. Of course, voices from different disciplines are essential but in the first instance the opinions and arguments of experts from this particular region could be more useful in understanding the situation. It is not so difficult to think of pragmatic reasons for political attempts to limit weapons supplies to Ukraine. As Ukrainian historian Kyrylo Tkachenko ironically observed: 'The Federal Republic of Germany is not a hippy commune but one of the largest arms producers in the world.'

I can also cite a number of protests in defence of democratic values where the pacifist approach had fatal consequences. Such as the recent incident in Belarus, where protesters fastidiously took off their shoes to stand on city benches to display their banners. The regime's terrifyingly bloody crackdown on these peaceful demonstrations is well known. Authoritarian rulers have no mercy, compassion, laws or respect for people who protest peacefully.

At the same time, the above passage from Yevgenia Belorusets' diary exposes the cunning of active supporters of pacifism—their formally reasonable but factually inapplicable arguments attack not the aggressor but the victims, who are merely trying to defend themselves in an unequal struggle. Particular concerns about the nature and relevance of expressions of pacifism in this situation inspire the relationship between pacifism as such and the law. After all, a concession to the territorial violations of the aggressor is contrary to the very logic of international law. Moreover, it plants a seed and sets a bad precedent that can support speculation on the resolution of future conflicts. The Russian Federation has attacked a sovereign state, as it has done many times before. Tolerating such a practice devalues the security structure, which means risking much more than just a few drops of sweat in your somewhat underheated living room. Giving in to the demands of aggressors does not lead to the conclusion of a stable peace, it merely creates a pause for reinforcements before a fresh attack.

Some Western pacifist slogans about military strategies in Ukraine make me reflect on why people subscribe to them. I think their position has to do with a sense of security and a sudden recognition of one's own vulnerability. In her recent essay 'On Vulnerability', Australian-born author and scholar McKenzie Wark perfectly describes the dangers of this particular type of vulnerability: 'The vulnerability of people who had expected to feel secure, who feel entitled to a predictable middle-class life, who imagine that vulnerability is something only other people are supposed to feel—that is a dangerous thing. It heightens a reflex that is probably always there but has become one of the main levers of the culture: to soothe unexpected vulnerability by attacking those even more vulnerable. In a word: fascism.'[3]

1

Yevgenia Belorusets, 'Letters from Kyiv. A Wartime Diary by Yevgenia Belorusets', 4 April 2022, www.artforum.com/slant/a-wartime-diary-by-yevgenia-belorusets-88035 (accessed 02/12/2022).

2

Kyrylo Tkachenko, 'Ziel und Mittel. Schwere Waffen für die Ukraine', 26 July 2022 ukraineverstehen.de/tkachenko-schwere-waffen-fuer-die-ukraine/ (accessed 02/12/2022).

3

McKenzie Wark, 'On Vulnerability', *SPIKE* 73 (Autumn 2022), p. 46–51.

BINARY INDIFFERENCE

Kyiv
Going to a play in Antwerp
Koksijde
23 March 2021
Autumn
Lisbon
On this day
Ohrid
At home
Beach days
Dnieper Reservoir

An algorithmic poem? A binary rhyme? On my smartphone, photo memories pop up daily. 'Memories', thematically compiled mini-photo albums of a sort. At first, I thought these appeared randomly. Over the past year, however, I have received a suspicious number of snapshots from Ukraine. That does leave a bit of a bitter taste. And it feels quite grim. Not really random, then, these automatic memories. Is my smartphone navigating the media interest in a country? Milking a bloody conflict? Algorithms know no decency.

You can hardly blame them, of course. Their indifference to war and peace, love and hate. Even life and death. Their innate passivity. Pardon, pre-programmed indifference. Just one option, between 1 and 0. That's hardly an ethical choice. Algorithms: unfeeling and apathetic decision-making machines. But more and more we let them lead and guide us. Has that no impact on our empathy? Or on our moral compass?

Nowadays, we are surrounded by a global network twenty-four hours a day. Our real life increasingly plays out in a symbolic universe of ones and zeros. Doesn't this affect our experience of that life, the meaning we give it? Algorithms don't distinguish between good and evil. Or between violent films and real-life violence. According to the London police, they even struggle to detect the

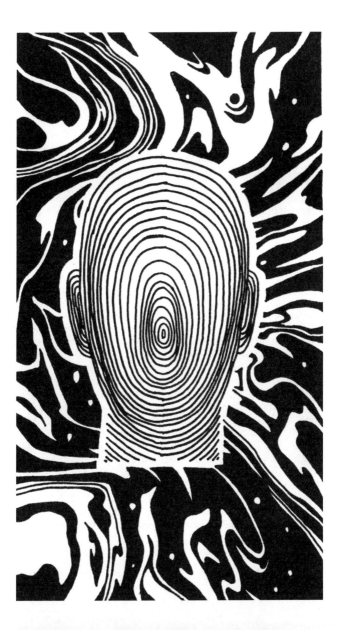

difference between child pornography and desert landscapes. So could they develop a moral code independently? A mathematical formula for ethics? Artificial intelligence for sensitive subjects?

Digital technologies and artificial intelligence lack the imagination for it. They can only encode sounds, images and movements logically. They can also record them meticulously and reproduce them vividly, but not interpret them to their heart's content. A digital camera can handle far more detail than a human brain. Millions of pixels, in fact—but a computer cannot draw half an ethical consequence from them. Does that exist, by the way? Half an ethic? A quantifiable morality?

Online memories have the inhuman ability to forget nothing. But they can't forgive anything or attribute blame to anything either. They owe their intelligence to gigabytes and connection speed. However—all the mega-memories, algorithms and meta-algorithms notwithstanding—we have artificial intelligence today, but no artificial intellectual yet. A human intellect is always plagued by a lack of memory. By gaps that need to be constantly filled. And that is done with imagination. A mixture of fact and fiction. Cognition and invention. An irrational choice is not necessarily a wrong choice, therefore. In the ratios of ones and zeros, affection and sentiment fall between the cracks. Without that, no morality. Without that, no fairness either. The play of ones and zeros creates the appearance of blind innocence. The veil of ignorance. Blind judgement and condemnation. An illusion of justice, in fact.

But judgement cannot be passed without touching. Nor without getting one's hands dirty. Situated knowledge. Saturated living. A sense of context and proportion. An intellectual exists only as an 'organic intellectual', as Antonio Gramsci once called them. But then I take that quite literally. A human being with organs and a body. Who has no choice but to fill the space between one and zero. Because they live with ambiguity, manipulation and murkiness. And they have a healthy suspicion of certainty and transparency for this very reason. An organic thinker sees through the clarity of a figure. Pierces the sincerity of a quota. Understands the illogicality in any logic. Has no artificially intelligent autism. Is not a mechanical intellectual. We meet those types all too often today at universities and on the Web of Science. Digital humanities or actually digital de-humanities? Algorithmic interpretations know neither consciousness nor conscience. A binary philosophy of life. An allergy to hybridism and ambiguity. Simultaneously immune to living between the lines. Or between legality and illegality. Implacable towards 'a-legality'. Science and ethics in quantity. True and false as a binary code. Good or bad as an exclusive choice. Black or white. Cancel culture, rejection, negation, deportation. With no intermediate ground, no grey area of residual misunderstanding. Blind judgement plus binary indifference: an explosive cocktail. Carelessly distributed between ones and zeros. Under the surface, something violent lurks within this binary brain.

DEHUMANISED SPACE

The unifying feature of collective action in support of 'peace at any cost' is the radical devaluation of Ukrainians' lives and of their aspirations, hopes and plans. All these human dimensions seem to have been lost. It is incredible how the supporters of this idea haven`t   tried to deepen their knowledge of, or at least unleash their imagination on, the Ukrainians forced to remain in the Russian-occupied territories. The latter are beyond the scope of the law. They risk their lives, health and property, lose their political and cultural rights, undergo humiliating purges and become targets of various forms of violence and discrimination. In such a paradigm, Ukraine itself is presented not as an independent state but as a kind of accumulation of resources, an area under one kind of control or another, a dehumanised space, an object. The creation of this image was facilitated by a multitude of prerequisites, a way of thinking that operates within a colonial framework. In it, the world is divided into developed independent countries, on the one hand, and developing countries that cannot govern themselves autonomously on the other. It makes the recent Russian invasion a very traumatic experience. One that rips open old wounds—wounds of which, in my view, the West has too little awareness.

Viewed from the cultural and political centres of the West, and from Moscow, Ukraine is seen as a periphery country. But the real position of the periphery is not measured in kilometres. From a central position of power, this space is seen as a lower stage of civilisation's development. Ukraine has huge economic resources but falls short in knowledge development. Stripped of the ability to approach the standard of the centre, the periphery cannot be 'contemporary' in this one-sided logic. If knowledge is generated at all, it is applied, and more suited to solving practical problems of production and exploitation. The country, its people and its natural resources are valued only in terms of economic possibilities, as a space that can potentially yield profit. Not as a cultural space that is home to living beings with their human sensitivities. The unique quality of Ukrainian soil in terms of agro-industry and mineral deposits has played a crucial role in this. Colonial logic did not consider the fate of the local population when it came to the development of the empire and the growth of its wealth. In Ukraine, this has taken radical forms on a number of occasions. One of the worst periods was when the criminal Stalinist machine created an artificial famine, the Holodomor. According to the most conservative estimates, it took 3.9 million lives. As a result of the criminal policy of collectivisation, which began in the mid-1920s, people were deprived of the right to own land. In 1932, the infamous Law of Spikelets came into effect. This law, which had no precedent in world history, allowed the state to seize unlimited amounts of grain from farms. Even taking a few spikelets—the remains of the plant after a field has been harvested—was considered theft. The methods employed by Russia today are just a continuation of this dehuman-ising geopolitics.

In the dark years of 1932–1933, Ukrainians fell into a deadly trap. Unrealistic plans for bread distribution or so-called grain confiscation condemned peasants to starvation. Any attempt to escape or to hide food was punished by confiscation of all their food or execution. Even a few ears of corn overwintering under the snow in a field were considered evidence of a crime. In fact, this law provided for immediate execution by shooting for theft of collective farm property or, as a milder sanction, the confiscation of the person's property. In extenuating circumstances, the punishment was ten years' imprisonment in the camps. Amnesty was prohibited. Under the laws of the time, the maximum penalty for deliberate manslaughter was up to ten years in prison. And theft of other people's property carried a maximum of three months' hard labour. Farmers were excluded from all market relations. It was forbidden to sell bread in the cities, and companies could not hire farmers. Along the western borders, blockade units shot refugees dead. Ukrainian villages were filled with party activists and organised teams whose task was to search for and seize food. At the same time, the USSR continued to export grain. This dark history still haunts millions of Ukrainian hearts to this day. It defines the country's cultural identity, its soul, its fears, its restlessness and its struggle.

As we witness an international constellation of parliaments recog-nising the Holodomor in Ukraine, it is easy to conclude that the non-recognition was a politicised position. During the current war, while Ukraine's agricultural infrastructure were being destroyed, grain fields set ablaze and seaports shelled, Russia, the true legitimate successor to the Soviet Union, has continued stubbornly with food speculation. The Black Sea Grain Initiative has allowed continuous supplies of Ukrainian grain to be exported abroad, although they still represent a fraction of pre-war quantities. At the same time, even under the sanctions, businesspeople and state-owned companies in Russia can still find routes to conduct an illegal trade of stolen grain through a shady system of sham companies, cargo manipulations and document forgeries.[1] This massive smuggling operation will surely be tried as a war crime. However, it is fascinating how the Kremlin still persists in conducting its criminal activities, even internationally. Foreign freight transportation is just one of the many areas it is involved in that is regulated by respected international organisations. Is it a bureaucratic clumsiness that prevents us from reacting quickly to such crimes even far from the war zone? Is the global regulatory system proving its inability to respond? Or is the continuation of the capitalist system more important than human bloodshed? Bureaucracy and capitalism certainly seem to be helping each other out quite nicely here.

The crimes of Stalinism have never been condemned by Russia and are sometimes not fully understood in the West. The official Russian historical narrative only gives space to Stalin's 'heroic deeds' and does not address the millions of victims of the bloody regime. The mythical portrait of Stalin that has been replicated for years by Putin's regime is that of a righteous and victorious leader under whom order prevailed in the country and who protected the Soviet people from the murderous Nazi army. By promoting the cult of power, accompanied as always by the cult of war, the regime has reinforced an old Russian tendency to confuse matters of the motherland with those of the monarch, as a famous Russian writer with German roots, Mikhail Saltykov-Shchedrin, pointed out as early as 1880.

1
Michael Biesecker, Sarah El Deeb and Beatrice Dupuy, 'Russia Smuggling Ukrainian Grain to Help Pay for Putin's War', 3 October 2022, apnews.com/article/russia-ukraine-putin-business-lebanon-syria-87c3b6fea3f4c326003123b21aa78099?utm_source=homepage&utm_medium=TopNews&utm_campaign=position_01 (accessed 02/12/2022).

PROPAGANDA

I never thought a war would persuade me to watch a television series. It feels a bit strange. Lounging on the couch for nights on end, with or without snacks, while the president of Ukraine entertains you. It's also a bit uncomfortable. After all, the chances that Netflix would have aired *Servant of the People*, starring Volodymyr Zelensky, without a Russian invasion seem quite slim to me. So the streaming platform owes this commercial success to Putin?

Although the satire addresses serious political issues, it hardly comes close to *Borgen*—that other highly successful political series that's also on Netflix—in terms of subtlety and nuance, or acting. While *Servant of the People* does manage to rise above the level of for instance *FC De Kampioenen*—a sitcom about a pub football team in Flanders—like the Flemish series, it is aimed at a local audience. And that audience was not targeted solely for commercial reasons. Zelensky clearly had another agenda. *Servant of the People* also became the name of the political party the actor went to the polls with in 2019. The series thus served as political propaganda. Was this premeditated?

That popular media such as film or television can make political careers, we already know from the examples of Ronald Reagan, Arnold Schwarzenegger and Silvio Berlusconi. So it's hardly surprising. What is surprising is that I was happy to let it suck me in pretty much every night. Mass media make you cynical. Something the German philosopher Peter Sloterdijk was well aware of forty years ago. The most gruesome images alternate with the most banal and frivolous news without batting an eyelid. That sort of thing generates collective resignation. On the primetime news of the Belgian public service TV channel, the 'main' news item, a cyclist's heroic victory, is followed immediately by evidently less important news. The rather less heroic images of massacred people in the streets of Ukraine. Unscrupulous.

Watching *Servant of the People* feels less harsh but feeds on the same shared mood: culturally embedded cynicism. I know I'm watching political propaganda. Also that the protagonist is currently in an inhumane situation, along with 'his' country. I am also well aware that Netflix is exploiting this magnificently. Still, I cannot help sitting here idly on my couch and laughing along. It is as if we park our critical minds alongside our worries about the world for a while. Just so we can still enjoy ourselves a little. A press of a button or a quick scroll is enough to step into another reality—to literally *divert* our thoughts. Perhaps it's no coincidence that the expression 'to divert one's thoughts' always points towards relaxation. The ideal mental gymnastics to escape stressful situations for a while. But also a media technique to keep the economy running. Business as usual. As Zelensky will know by now, being a true servant of the people, like war, protest or activism, is not very lucrative. Making television is.

THE AESTHETICS OF TRUST

There is at least one thing that nationalist politicians share with modern artists. They both pride themselves on their autonomy. Vasily Goloborodko, alias Zelensky—invariably spelt with a 'y' since the war, because Zelenski with an 'i' looks pro-Russian and therefore not very autonomous—makes a point of honour of it in *Servant of the People*. Clean up corruption! Get rid of oligarchs, but also any IMF interference. Autonomy, not only to give pride back to the Ukrainian people, but also to give them power 'again'. That 'again' is in inverted commas because the question is whether the people have ever had any power. And, for the record, by that I don't just mean the Ukrainian people, but any people living in a representative democracy. I don't know of any countries where the people are truly in power: states with direct democracy. In fact, according to most political scientists and experts, such a thing is impossible. True self-government or real autonomy is only possible on a very small scale. For communities of up to fifty members, apparently. So that won't work for a state, let alone for Europe. It may sound strange but, at that scale, autonomous government means that the government can actually decide independently of its own people. Within a parliamentary democracy, the opposition can challenge decisions, but even that criticism can only be raised on behalf of the people and not by the people. Of course, there are always politicians who claim to speak for the people, but they are best viewed with some suspicion. Populism, you know. No matter how democratic a policy is, the gap between citizens and government will always be there. Indeed, it must continue to be there, precisely for the sake of democracy. Distance is needed for fairness. Some distrust towards politicians who claim to close this gap is therefore recommended. Calls for 'active citizenship' often sound like a power grab from conservative circles. But closing the gap even in good faith would pose some interesting governance problems. Imagine if any citizen could storm into parliament to question any decision. The political decision-making machine would soon grind to a halt. And it already does so often enough today without any assistance. Even without switched-on citizens.

Autonomy in a well-run democracy, therefore, paradoxically presupposes that the people keep their mouths shut from time to time. Representative governance simply requires consent and thus also a relatively *passive* electorate. For a time, at least. Activism may well be a democratic right, but passivity is a democratic good. Indeed, in a representative democracy, the latter is a sign of trust. The trust that those you voted for will make the right decisions, or at least that they will accomplish their mission with the best intentions and in the public interest.

In *Servant of the People*, Goloborodko also relies on passivity and blind faith. To guarantee an autonomous government, he tries to escape the influence of the oligarchs. The path he takes to achieve this is remarkable. Following the rules for 'good governance', he tries to recruit the most capable ministers through open vacancies and examinations, like in business. In the satire, that plan is thwarted by manipulative oligarchs. But could such an equitable procedure actually put a credible government in office? In today's expertocracy, open vacancies and transparent procedures will certainly build trust. The transparency rhetoric might also work for a technocracy. However, it scarcely works for a democracy. There, trust is built in a completely different way. This became crystal clear in Goloborodko's second attempt to form a government.

After his failed attempt to put together a credible team, he boldly appoints a few old friends as ministers, including his ex-wife. In Belgium, we would call that blatant nepotism. Moreover, the political competence of some of the newly appointed government members is questionable. It all reeks of corruption. Yet the new president gets away with it. Despite fierce media criticism. Why? Perhaps because trust is based on a lack of transparency. It is not with open vacancies and objective procedures that confidence is generated. Instead, trust is created in a rather murky *atmosphere* of trust. Equally blinding is the 'ray' with which someone radiates trust. An atmosphere is difficult to substantiate, and a 'ray' of this sort is difficult to measure. Trust is therefore built not only on what people say or do but also on *how* they say or do it. Trust now relies on presence, appearance or image, and on rhetoric and performance quality. I call this the 'aesthetics of trust'. Generating trust is an artistic skill. Gaining trust is an art, at the very least a performing art, but to some extent also a *visual* art. Which, as we know, offers acceptance through acknowledgement. Familiarity breeds confidence. Speak the language of the streets, crack the jokes of the average Jo(e). Make the faces that people know. Use the gestures people are used to. Act as expected! And, if you really want to do something unexpected, then do the *expected* unexpected. Read: be 'common'! Even vulgar. And speak authoritatively, preferably somewhat indignantly or disdainfully. Donald Trump, Silvio Berlusconi or Bart De Wever. Both the mass media and populism benefit from it.

Still, the aesthetics of trust need not necessarily be vulgar. Trust can just as easily be won with style. Style, certainly. Not just words, but voice; not just content, but form. Together, they inspire confidence. This is certainly true for the mass public and a national electorate that has to vote for an as yet unknown candidate. An aspiring politician cannot yet be judged on deeds. Promises have yet to be fulfilled. There's no hard evidence. Just credentials. Indeed, you can but give *credence* to unproven promises. That applies as much to God as to the budding politician. And equally as much to something as vague as nation and homeland. You can but have blind faith in it. But once that credence, that faith, is there, something magical happens. It works just like religion. Faith creates faith. Confidence begets confidence. A veritable alchemy of faith and confidence: a confidant gains the power to convince others to have confidence in their confidants too. A king, parliament or president has confidence in the government. Goloborodko has confidence in his old friends. German sociologist Niklas Luhmann, with his slightly irritating tautology, would perhaps call such a thing a 'confiding confidence' or a 'trusting trust'. The confidant's halo radiates confidence over their own confidants, causing the electorate to also have confidence in the latter. *Good* governance relies on transparency and procedural activity, *autonomous* governance on trust and compliant passivity. The former is the work of a manager, the latter of an artist. And politicians? They waver somewhere between the two. But if politics becomes a marriage of art and management, it is high time to find an escape route.

GREAT RUSSIAN PASSIVITY

On 14 April 2022, Russian opposition leader Alexei Navalny, currently a 'prisoner of conscience', tweeted: 'One shot from Javelin costs $230,000. For the same money we would get 200 million ad views in different formats and provide at least 300,000 link clicks or at least 8 million views on a video with the truth about what is happening in Ukraine.' And he continued: 'Even if such advertising is bought for the full commercial price, its cost will be laughable compared to the price of this war.' This idea, which at first sight seems practical and even pacifist, embodies the old imperialist technique of translating the real into the symbolic. The opposition leader's proposal to save Ukraine suggests that the Russians are unaware of the heinous crimes they are committing there. If they were to find out, he implies, they would undoubtedly take up arms against the regime. Advertisements, in other words, will save everyone. Navalny's statement initially seemed to me to be a sincere search for a solution. In reality, however, it promotes the notion that the majority of Russians are 'fundamentally ignorant', and that is at odds with reality. The problem with the Russian majority lies precisely in the fact that, knowing what is happening in Ukraine, it continues to support the government and justify the government's actions to itself.

In September, after the announcement of mobilisation, an opinion poll on Russian attitudes towards the war showed some change since the invasion. Those who 'definitely' or 'mostly' support the invasion fell from 81% to 75%, and those who mostly or definitely do not support it rose from 14% to 20%.[1] These minimal changes can scarcely make a difference. In a recent interview with Bloomberg, representatives of the Levada Center, the largest independent opinion centre in Russia, explained why hopes that Russians will oppose the war have been dashed. First of all, passivity and indifference: 'The boss knows best, his opinion is my opinion; I do not want war, but Putin had nowhere else to go—NATO was at the gate.' A propaganda-fuelled majority justifies the regime's actions as a 'pre-emptive strike', 'an unavoidable measure', 'defence against NATO', or a desire to protect what Russians describe as 'Ukraine's

Russian-speaking population'. Some respondents, especially women and younger people, engaged in a form of self-persuasion, claiming, for example: 'There was no choice,' or 'No, you can't be in favour of war. Our soldiers are being killed there, and Ukrainian soldiers too, and civilians, and children. But what other choice was there? Who can say what other choice there was? Negotiate with them? It was too late!' Are those the words of people who don't know what's going on?

The political and mental passivity of the vast Russian majority is rooted not only in a slavish sense of existential hopelessness, but also in the poisonous imperialist belief that Russians cannot ever be in the wrong. They continue to defend this idea with multiple, but still flimsy, arguments: because Russia is so big, or the 'great Russian culture' (which is so often built on copying Western practices) is so impossibly valuable; or with facile decisions proposed by the Russian orthodox church—there is no end to the excuses they may find. Each criminal seizure of foreign territories meets with support among the population as far as it confirms their delusions. Real crimes are transferred to the symbolic value of the Russian soul's charm. This is proved not only by the experiences of their victims and observers but by the dry stats—for what the latter are still worth, of course.

That is also why I dare to warn against so-called Russian dissidents being allowed to travel too easily within Europe today. After all, in reality they are simply looking for a more comfortable life than that offered by sanctioned Russia. Finnish Prime Minister Sanna Marin's stance on the EU ban on tourist visas for Russian citizens has therefore found wide resonance. 'It's not right that at the same time as Russia is waging an aggressive, brutal war of aggression in Europe, Russians can live a normal life, travel in Europe, be tourists. It's not right.' A similar attitude is endorsed by countries that experienced the horrors of Soviet occupation, such as the Baltic countries, Poland and the Czech Republic.

On this issue, I think it is valuable to listen to the views of those directly affected by Russia's actions. Often, those protesting against stopping cooperation with the Russians are Western journalists, politicians and intellectuals who have only ever seen Russian tanks in photographs. Or they've been on a week-long 'crazy Eastern European trip', and now they pretend to be regional experts. So let me recall the reaction of the Georgians. They have just suffered a Russian military invasion. Last autumn, they were startled by crowds of Russians arriving, fleeing mobilisation. The Georgians have experienced first-hand how this mechanism works. First the Russian language takes its place in society and then tanks are driven in under the pretext that 'here the Russian-speaking population is being discriminated against'. Georgian border guards systematically put arriving Russians through a polygraph. Of course, the device is highly controversial, but the unwillingness to see supporters of the 'Russian world' in the country carries more weight. When Georgians see groups of Russian deserters, they greet them with 'Glory to Ukraine!'

I remember how the aforementioned Russian opposition leader Navalny often used the derogatory nickname 'rodents' for Georgians in 2008, saying that they were uninhibited and needed to be tamed. In other words, the poison of imperialism permeates the whole of Russian society, knowing neither class, profession, nor phantom differences in political views. It is highly unpleasant to watch how former beneficiaries of Russian cultural budgets become welcome guests at European cultural forums when, at the same time, they immediately make very dubious statements. One striking example is the Russian director Kirill Serebrennikov, sustained by state and oligarchic support in Russia. In 2020, Serebrennikov was convicted of fraud in Russia and ordered to pay Russia's culture ministry 129 million roubles in compensation. The director did not have the money, but oligarch Roman Abramovich agreed to pay his debt. Now watch my hands: having escaped to France in March 2022, Serebrennikov went straight to work at the Cannes Film Festival. Partly thanks to some generous help from Abramovich. Speaking at the festival, Serebrennikov called for the lifting of sanctions on this oligarch. Of course, exported cultural products are a tool of both the Russian defence ministry and oligarchic structures. But what is so attractive about this country's cultural heritage? What is the reason for this 'greatness'? After all, the qualifier 'great' in relation to culture is not used very often. We hardly ever hear statements such as 'great American culture' or 'great Dutch culture'. Consequently, strategies to promote Russia's cultural product tend not to focus on artistic goals at all. Russia's aim is to assert its superiority on the cultural map. Budgets for presenting Russian culture with state and oligarchic origins have always been incomparably larger than those of other Eastern European countries. It reinforces the impression that Russia is the only important partner. Nevertheless, the same budgets still operate in Europe today, supported by calls not to boycott the 'great Russian culture'. Just recently, for instance, Brussels' Rue du Méridien in Schaerbeek was host to the photographic exhibition 'Russian Civilisation', designed to glorify the cultural diversity of the country's peoples. On display were the finalists in a competition of the same name. The contest was established under the Russian Federation's state programme 'Implementation of State National Policy', and its nominations included headings such as 'Spiritual Ties' and 'Family Values'. This took place while coffins continue to stream out of Ukraine to Buryatia. For comparison, Russians from Moscow die in the war in Ukraine 87.5 times less often than Dagestanis, 275 times less than Buryats and 350 times less than Tuvans. Russia is using the war as a pretext for purges among its non-Slavic population. Ethnocide, in other words.

Russians are silent, and only rare cases of resistance surface, mostly among non-Slavic peoples colonised by Russia. The majority is convinced that the war will not affect them directly. A substantial part of the Russian intelligentsia, including the so-called liberals, is a useless and incompetent elite that for years has avoided any direct contact with 'ordinary people'. They continue to call for a deeper look into the incomprehensible Russian soul and are full of admiration for their cultural products. The result is that focus shifts again from the real to the symbolic.

1
Tobin Harshaw, 'How Does Putin Stay So Popular While Losing the War in Ukraine? A Q&A with Russian polling experts Denis Volkov and Andrei Kolesnikov on tracking public opinion in Russia', 1 October 2022, www.bloomberg.com/opinion/articles/2022-10-01/why-do-so-many-russians-still-support-putin-s-ukraine-war?leadSource=uverify%20wall (accessed 02/12/2022).

THE POLITICS OF FEAR

Fear of failure.
Fear of the virus. Fear of germs.
Terror and terrorism.
Egophobia: fear of being a nobody, of not meaning anything.
Relationship anxiety: fear of losing a partner. Fear of not finding
a partner. On the shelf in your thirties.
Fear of losing status or, conversely, imposter syndrome for
status climbers.
Fear of unemployment. Loss of income.
Fear of reputational damage.
Fear of competitors.
Stock market hysteria: fear of losing capital.
Fear of being bullied.
Fat phobia: fear of putting on weight.
Fear of the Other: Islamophobia, xenophobia, homophobia,
even gynophobia.
Climate anxiety: water shortage or conversely flooding, also fires.
And finally: fear of death.

According to German sociologist Heinze Bude, we live in a society
of fear. People huddle together like packs of nervous scaredy-cats.
That's how I imagine it, at least. Although humans no more live in
packs than cats do. Instead, they live together less and less, although
they do live in fear. Because fear individualises, isolates, psycholo-
gises and polarises. Fearfulness simultaneously produces common
enemies and solitary beings. Despite living in prosperous Europe.

     The richer people are, the more fearful they are. You could
call that the fear paradox. And here is another: the safer people are,
the greater their subjective sense of threat. Code red, from an initial
orange. Danger lurks around every corner. Phobocracy as a new
governance model? That brings me to the prevailing culture of safety
and security. From safe transport to the Safety Council. No house

without its fire alarm. From safe education to safe space. From social security to life insurance. No festival or school building without security. More police on the streets. More cameras in the streets. Neighbourhood watch WhatsApp groups. Everyone in SUVs. To the point of absurdity: *Veilig leren lezen*—literally translated: 'safely learn to read' is a successful Dutch textbook for our primary school children. Could language present a threat? Contagious diseases? Dirty words, perhaps? Certainly hurtful words.

The cult of security as the opium of the society of fear. As we know, a belief of this kind craves leadership, and authoritarian and conservative policies. The preservation of what we have. Not offensive policies but defensive ones. Prevention and defence first and foremost. A social psychosis of fear vitalises not only a strange kind of authority but also collective passivity. Possibly even a general inability to function. Social paralysis. Just as a witness to street violence or a bank robbery may be confounded, for a time entire societies stood paralysed watching the war.

Paralysis, wasn't that Europe's first reflex response to the Russian threat, as well as Ukraine's? First denial, then disbelief, then general paralysis. My Ukrainian colleagues were stunned to see their government ignore warnings from NATO and the United States. I myself was equally stunned when the same NATO and Europe did not intervene when the invasion became a reality. The 'free' West seemed afflicted by indecision at its deepest core. Why was there no military intervention? Not even a no-fly zone. Economic sanctions came hesitantly at first. Sometimes in the form of half-hearted measures. What was the cause of all this procrastination? Fear of repercussions. Worries about conflict escalation. Pouring oil on the flames. Even a threat of the Bomb. And then the most opportunistic rationale of all: an intervention would impact the European economy. Eventually hit citizens' wallets too. Or this distasteful reasoning in Belgium: a boycott of the Russian diamond trade would let other diamond-trading countries reap all the profits. Fear of recession combined with fear of competition. Meanwhile, we could feel the effects in our pockets. All to no avail.

What conviction was behind this non-interventionist diplomacy? Peace as a miraculous side effect of the globalised market economy? International trade relations generate global dependency relationships too. The same logic behind the creation of the European Union, initially an *economic* union. Capitalism as the spreader of world peace. We know the result. A grim pacifism for a privileged area. Social peace and prosperity as problems are sweated out and fought elsewhere. European peace at the expense of the rest of the world. Preaching pacifism so that violence and misery do not come here. Better in the neighbours' backyard. And easing our conscience with refugee shelters and benefit shows. Pity-based solidarity in heavily promoted passion plays. Could there be a sacred alliance between pacifism, passivity and compassion? A deeply embedded European Christian tradition?

In Gandhi's distinction between freedom from violence and non-violence, the European Union seems to have opted for the latter ever since its creation. Many tactical and pragmatic considerations. Not so much because of any fundamental convictions. Is that not advocating peace out of fear and weakness? Certainly very little bravery. The politics of fear, wavering between pacifism and indifference.

WORDS

During my stay in Ukraine a record number of deaths occurred. The highest since the start of the so-called 'full-scale' invasion. A thousand each day. Thousands of lives, thousands of maimed families, thousands of traumatized souls. For life. For many, no more life.

The same week, more than 350,000 German citizens, including prominent artists and intellectuals such as Katharina Thalbach and Peter Weibel, signed a *Manifest für Frieden* (Manifesto for Peace). Against arms supply and for compromise. The initiative came from feminist Alice Schwarzer and Die Linke politician Sahra Wagenknecht. Their argument: fear of escalation, fear of the Bomb. At the same time, the slogan 'Nicht unser Krieg' (Not Our War) dominates Berlin streets. When I ask Ukrainian artists, academics, feminists, activists, soldiers and ordinary citizens about the meaning of this Western pacifism, I see disbelief, bewilderment, anger, tears.

You can break a people with weapons, but also with words. While Ukrainian cities are under heavy artillery fire from the east, the morale of a population is being undermined with well-meaning pacifism from the west.

Whichever camp you choose, the dispute makes at least one thing clear. Besides a bloody conflict, a culture war is raging in Europe. Besides weapons, words matter. Not only the letters and manifestos of Western pacifists testify to this. The handbooks sent to schools immediately after the Russian occupation of Kherson also underline the importance of words. A rewritten history. Neat for every school year. We all recognise it by now. What this Russian book post makes especially clear: there is more than just a bilateral conflict going on here. Politicians and leading figures such as Lula da Silva and Pope Francis may still want to believe otherwise. Even the German manifesto writers still seem to assume it.

A compromise is something that is reached between two sides. However, this war is not bilateral, but imperial. The latter adjective implies a colonial struggle. Such a struggle is both territorial and cultural. Therefore, a compromise would not only involve annexing Crimea and perhaps some more square kilometres.

Culturally, all of Ukraine would remain in Moscow's grip. After all, Putin today casts himself as the defender of the great Russian culture, of Pushkin, Tchaikovsky and Tolstoy. In the process, the culture of the former USSR countries has been denigrated as inferior for decades. This is precisely why we must understand the Ukrainian resistance as a decolonialization struggle. The stakes of such a fight? To let people know that Ukraine exists. That a Ukrainian culture breathes and lives. That the ballerinas Edwar Degas painted were not Russian but Ukrainian in origin. This may be a battle that is far less bloody than the current war of positions. But one that is much more complex and fragile.

In Kyiv, two friends told me that they had deliberately stopped speaking Russian to each other for several months now, despite the fact that it was the language they were most familiar with, their way of having everyday talks as well as difficult conversations. Their way of sharing feelings. Their way of being themselves. Now all that is no longer possible or desirable. That's how it feels to them anyway. But can you just cut a culture out of your own country, out of your own body, out of your own being? Is it possible to decolonialize your own being? Amputate your personality? What gaping wounds will remain? Is it enough to bury a language and a few symbols? Banish a few works of art? Even rewrite an entire history? More than a century of Russian occupation doesn't just erase itself.

When politicians and journalists talk about reconstruction, they mostly talk about economy and infrastructure. But something like that takes a decade all in all. On a cultural level, the wounds cut much deeper, the traumas last for generations. These can hit back a society like a boomerang even after decades. Also politics and economics, nature and life. Who will heal those wounds? How to plug those holes?

When pacifists talk about compromise, they think primarily of diplomatic and territorial agreements. Sometimes they do think of their own security and comfort as well. 'Abstract pacifism' is what my feminist friends in Ukraine call it. Colonial politics, however, is immune to borders and territory, to walls and barbed wire. It is about mental terror, brainwashing and indoctrination. It is about undermining the power of all the Ukrainian people to give things meaning. The opportunities to give meaning to your own life and to the society you live in. Those possibilities are still largely determined by Russia to this day, as it has in fact been doing so for more than a hundred years. With the war, Ukraine's awareness of that cultural manipulation has grown enormously. This is partly why it does not want a compromise. It will not fall into the same trap of the past. Forcing a compromise today is simply asking for Ukrainian capitulation.

We can think along with the pacifists. We can argue with them and argue against them. I enjoy doing it. Every night—with or without a glass of wine. But you can't argue with brute force. With rapists and murderers, Ukraine does not want to compromise. No more. Never again. Against weapons, not even verbal violence helps. To war one can only respond with war. This perhaps, paradoxically, to recover some pacifism later on. Perhaps one of an entirely different nature. This time not abstract, but concrete pacifism. For Europe, including Ukraine.

As I write this, I am standing at the Ukrainian-Polish border. Men like me are viewed with suspicion. Men who want to flee Ukraine are plucked from trains. This is the truth of every war. Geopolitical as well as gender-specific. War is always also culturally determined. Words matter.

ACKNOWLEDGEMENTS

Alexandra Tryanova:
Special thanks to Nikolay Karabinovych.

Pascal Gielen:
Thank you Liesbeth, Ono and Milan.

Polina Frank:
Thanks to Kevin, Bee and the whole team of Mosel Mosel who made me feel like home in the Netherlands.
Thanks to the Armed Forces of Ukraine, including my brother Dima who keep fighting for the existence and liberty of my homeland.

SOURCES

'My Country' is written by Alexandra Tryanova and Pascal Gielen
'Societal Fatigue' is written by Pascal Gielen
'Not a Hippy Commune' is written by Alexandra Tryanova
'Binary Indifference' is written by Pascal Gielen
'Dehumanised Space' is written by Alexandra Tryanova
'Propaganda' is written by Pascal Gielen
'The Aesthetics of Trust' is written by Pascal Gielen
'Great Russian Passivity' is written by Alexandra Tryanova
'The Politics of Fear' is written by Pascal Gielen
'Words' is written by Pascal Gielen

Some parts of Pascal Gielen's text were previously published:
• 'Words' appeared in *De Standaard*, on 17 February 2023, original title: 'Je kunt een volk met wapens breken, en met woorden' [You can break a People with Weapons, and with Words].
• 'The Politics of Fear' was published in *De Morgen* on 7 February 2023, original title: 'Geen vrede voor elke prijs' [No Peace at Any Cost].
• 'Propaganda' was published in *De Morgen* on 31 August 2022.

AUTHORS

Alexandra Tryanova (1990, Odesa, UA) is an independent curator. She focuses on contemporary practices relating to gender, institutional critique and Eastern European avant-gardes. Alexandra Tryanova holds Master's degrees in Cultural Studies and Law, and in 2022 she has graduated from the KASK Curatorial Studies programme. Recently she was involved in projects at Kunsthal Extra City, Antwerp and Jester, Genk. Previously she held the position of curator at the Museum of Odesa Modern Art (2018/19) and junior curator at the PinchukArtCentre, Kyiv (2019/21). Since 2017 she runs an independent non-production residency Kunsthalle Lustdorf, based on temporary independent artistic and curatorial associations for open practices and technologies in the area of the Green Valley in the suburbs of Odesa.

Pascal Gielen (1970, BE) is a sociologist of culture, focusing on the political and social context of creative labour. He is based at the Antwerp Research Institute for the Arts (ARIA) of the Antwerp University, where he leads the research group Culture Commons Quest Office (CCQO). In 2016 Gielen was the recipient of the Odysseus Grant for excellent international research by the Fonds Wetenschappelijk Onderzoek (Fund for Scientific Research). Gielen is editor of the book series Antennae-Arts in Society (Valiz, Amsterdam). He has published over a dozen books on art, creative labour, and cultural politics.

Visuals
Polina Frank (2000, Dnipro, UA) created the drawings for this publication. Her work is characterised by a psychedelic, geometric style. She studied journalism and communication (University of Vienna). Simultaneously with her studies, she developed her artistic practice and started tattooing. Since the outbreak of the war, she has been active as a voluntary supplier of military equipment to the Ukrainian armed forces. Polina currently travels back and forth between the Netherlands and Ukraine and combines her volunteer work with tattooing and other artistic work. At the end of 2022, she had a solo exhibition in Kiyv and participated in a group exhibition at Monopole Gallery in Berlin.

PASSIVITY
Between Indifference and Pacifism

Authors
Alexandra Tryanova
Pascal Gielen

Visuals
Polina Frank
Passivity, 2023,
ink drawings on paper
*Polina Frank's work was included on
recommendation of the publisher.*

Project editor
Simone Wegman/Valiz

Copy-editing
Els Brinkman

Translation (Du-En)
KennisTranslations
(Caroline Durant)

Design
Lotte Lara Schröder
@speculativepress
HAL Timezone by HAL Typefaces
VTC TATSURO by Vocal Type

Publisher
Valiz, Amsterdam, 2023
www.valiz.nl

Paper inside
Munken Print White, 100 gr 1.5

Paper cover
Munken Print White, 300 gr 1.5

Lithography
Mariska Bijl, Wilco Art Books,
Amersfoort

Printing
Wilco Art Books, Amersfoort

Distribution
NL: Centraal Boekhuis, www.cb.nl
BE: Epo, www.epo.be
USA/Canada/Latin America: D.A.P., www.artbook.com
GB/IE: Central Books, www.anagrambooks.com
Europe/Asia: Idea Books, www.ideabooks.nl
Australia: Perimeter Books, www.perimeterdistribution.com

THIS PUBLICATION WAS MADE POSSIBLE THROUGH THE GENEROUS SUPPORT OF

– Antwerp Research Institute for the Arts (ARIA), Antwerp

ARIA
Antwerp Research Institute for the Arts
University of Antwerp

– Support Fund for Ukranian Artists (an initiative of the Dutch Ministry of Education, Culture and Science (OCW) and the Ministry of Foreign Affairs (BZ). The programme is administered by the Dutch Foundation for Literature, in collaboration with other Dutch national cultural foundations (Mondriaan Fund, Netherlands Film Fund, Creative Industries Fund NL, Performing Arts Fund NL and Cultural Participation Fund).

Nederlands
letterenfonds
dutch foundation
for literature

This publication has also been published in Dutch:

PASSIVITEIT
Tussen onverschilligheid en pacifisme
ISBN 978-94-93246-23-2, Valiz, 2023.

This English edition:
ISBN 978-94-93246-22-5
Printed and bound in the Netherlands/EU

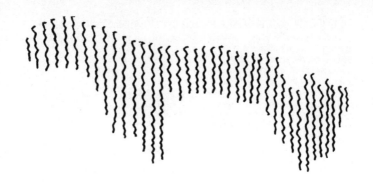

PREVIOUSLY PUBLISHED:

Marlies De Munck & Pascal Gielen
Fragility: To Touch and Be Touched
ISBN 978-94-93246-10-2, Valiz, 2022.

Marlies De Munck & Pascal Gielen
Kwetsbaarheid: Over raken en geraakt worden
ISBN 978-94-93246-09-6, Valiz, 2022.

Marlies De Munck & Pascal Gielen
Nearness: Art and Education after Covid-19
ISBN 978-94-92095-86-2, Valiz, 2020.

Marlies De Munck & Pascal Gielen
Nabijheid: Kunst en onderwijs na Covid-19
ISBN 978-94-92095-87-9, Valiz, 2020.